About Skill Builders Subtraction

by R. B. Snow and Clareen Nelson-Arnold

Welcome to RBP Books' Skill Builders series. Like our Summer Bridge Activities collection, the Skill Builders series is designed to make learning both fun and rewarding.

Skill Builders Subtraction provides students with focused practice to help reinforce and develop subtraction skills. Each Skill Builders volume is grade-level appropriate with clear examples and instructions on each page to guide the lesson. In accordance with NCTM standards, exercises include a variety of activities to help students develop their ability to work with numbers in a subtraction format.

A critical thinking section includes exercises to develop higher-order thinking skills.

Learning is more effective when approached with an element of fun and enthusiasm—just as most children approach life. That's why the Skill Builders combine entertaining and academically sound exercises and fun themes to make reviewing basic skills fun and effective, for both you and your budding scholars.

Table of Contents

Problem Solving

Write the difference.

1.

10	4	6	9	8
-1	-4	-0	-6	-2
9				

2.

5	11	2	5	10
-4	-0	-1	-2	-4

3.

12	10	7	6	11
-2	-8	-2	-3	-5

4.

6	11	1	5	12
-2	-2	-0	-4	-7

5.

12	7	0	2	10
-0	-3	-0	-2	-7

Write the difference.

1.

$$\begin{array}{r} 9 \\ -1 \\ \hline \mathbf{8} \end{array} \qquad \begin{array}{r} 10 \\ -5 \\ \hline \end{array} \qquad \begin{array}{r} 7 \\ -4 \\ \hline \end{array} \qquad \begin{array}{r} 6 \\ -6 \\ \hline \end{array} \qquad \begin{array}{r} 8 \\ -0 \\ \hline \end{array}$$

2.

$$\begin{array}{r} 7 \\ -7 \\ \hline \end{array} \qquad \begin{array}{r} 4 \\ -3 \\ \hline \end{array} \qquad \begin{array}{r} 10 \\ -3 \\ \hline \end{array} \qquad \begin{array}{r} 6 \\ -4 \\ \hline \end{array} \qquad \begin{array}{r} 3 \\ -3 \\ \hline \end{array}$$

3.

$$\begin{array}{r} 9 \\ -3 \\ \hline \end{array} \qquad \begin{array}{r} 10 \\ -6 \\ \hline \end{array} \qquad \begin{array}{r} 12 \\ -4 \\ \hline \end{array} \qquad \begin{array}{r} 5 \\ -3 \\ \hline \end{array} \qquad \begin{array}{r} 6 \\ -5 \\ \hline \end{array}$$

4.

$$\begin{array}{r} 8 \\ -2 \\ \hline \end{array} \qquad \begin{array}{r} 11 \\ -7 \\ \hline \end{array} \qquad \begin{array}{r} 9 \\ -4 \\ \hline \end{array} \qquad \begin{array}{r} 6 \\ -3 \\ \hline \end{array} \qquad \begin{array}{r} 8 \\ -5 \\ \hline \end{array}$$

5.

$$\begin{array}{r} 7 \\ -5 \\ \hline \end{array} \qquad \begin{array}{r} 8 \\ -1 \\ \hline \end{array} \qquad \begin{array}{r} 9 \\ -5 \\ \hline \end{array} \qquad \begin{array}{r} 12 \\ -3 \\ \hline \end{array} \qquad \begin{array}{r} 11 \\ -9 \\ \hline \end{array}$$

Problem Solving

Write the difference.

1.

10 − 0 = __10__

5 − 1 = _____

11 − 3 = _____

10 − 2 = _____

2 − 0 = _____

4 − 1 = _____

2.

7 − 1 = _____

12 − 9 = _____

8 − 5 = _____

9 − 9 = _____

3 − 2 = _____

5 − 0 = _____

3.

8 − 6 = _____

12 − 11 = _____

1 − 1 = _____

9 − 5 = _____

10 − 3 = _____

9 − 2 = _____

4.

6 − 0 = _____

11 − 8 = _____

8 − 8 = _____

12 − 2 = _____

10 − 10 = _____

7 − 5 = _____

I bet you can do this exercise in a snap!

Problem Solving

Write the difference.

1.

$11 - 1 =$ __**10**__

$9 - 7 =$ _____

$8 - 3 =$ _____

$10 - 3 =$ _____

$12 - 12 =$ _____

$9 - 0 =$ _____

2.

$3 - 0 =$ _____

$11 - 4 =$ _____

$9 - 8 =$ _____

$1 - 1 =$ _____

$11 - 6 =$ _____

$9 - 2 =$ _____

3.

$11 - 11 =$ _____

$10 - 9 =$ _____

$12 - 3 =$ _____

$4 - 0 =$ _____

$7 - 3 =$ _____

$8 - 1 =$ _____

4.

$4 - 2 =$ _____

$12 - 5 =$ _____

$8 - 4 =$ _____

$5 - 5 =$ _____

$9 - 2 =$ _____

$11 - 10 =$ _____

6

Start with 49. Write backwards to 0.

49									
									0

1.   What number comes before 47? _____

2.   What number comes before 11? _____

3.   What number comes between 27 and 29? _____

4.   What number comes after 32? _____

Start with 99. Write backwards to 50.

99									
									50

1. What are the even numbers between 50 and 60?

50 _____ _____ _____ _____ 60.

2. What are the odd numbers between 81 and 91?

81 _____ _____ _____ _____ 91.

3. What is the next even number after 64? _____

Problem Solving

Solve each problem below.

1.
$$\begin{array}{r} 7 \\ -4 \\ \hline \textbf{3} \end{array}$$
$$\begin{array}{r} 7 \\ -0 \\ \hline \end{array}$$
$$\begin{array}{r} 10 \\ -8 \\ \hline \end{array}$$
$$\begin{array}{r} 4 \\ -4 \\ \hline \end{array}$$
$$\begin{array}{r} 3 \\ -2 \\ \hline \end{array}$$

2.
$$\begin{array}{r} 11 \\ -8 \\ \hline \end{array}$$
$$\begin{array}{r} 8 \\ -1 \\ \hline \end{array}$$
$$\begin{array}{r} 9 \\ -2 \\ \hline \end{array}$$
$$\begin{array}{r} 6 \\ -2 \\ \hline \end{array}$$
$$\begin{array}{r} 4 \\ -1 \\ \hline \end{array}$$

3.
$$\begin{array}{r} 9 \\ -7 \\ \hline \end{array}$$
$$\begin{array}{r} 0 \\ -0 \\ \hline \end{array}$$
$$\begin{array}{r} 4 \\ -1 \\ \hline \end{array}$$
$$\begin{array}{r} 8 \\ -2 \\ \hline \end{array}$$
$$\begin{array}{r} 9 \\ -1 \\ \hline \end{array}$$

4.
$$\begin{array}{r} 6 \\ -2 \\ \hline \end{array}$$
$$\begin{array}{r} 1 \\ -1 \\ \hline \end{array}$$
$$\begin{array}{r} 7 \\ -3 \\ \hline \end{array}$$
$$\begin{array}{r} 6 \\ -0 \\ \hline \end{array}$$
$$\begin{array}{r} 12 \\ -1 \\ \hline \end{array}$$

5.
$$\begin{array}{r} 12 \\ -9 \\ \hline \end{array}$$
$$\begin{array}{r} 5 \\ -1 \\ \hline \end{array}$$
$$\begin{array}{r} 10 \\ -6 \\ \hline \end{array}$$
$$\begin{array}{r} 7 \\ -3 \\ \hline \end{array}$$
$$\begin{array}{r} 10 \\ -2 \\ \hline \end{array}$$

Word Problem Solving

Read the story. Write the problem and the answer.

1. LeeAnn fed the neighbors' dogs while they were on a trip. She fed 9 dogs in the morning and only 7 dogs at night. How many dogs did not eat at night?

9 – 7 = 2 dogs

2. Denise planted 5 roses in her flower garden. 3 roses were red. The rest of them were pink. How many roses were pink?

_____

3. 10 nuts were on the ground. The chipmunks ate 7 of them. How many nuts were left on the ground?

_____

4. Tanner got a new box of 12 crayons. 6 of them were broken. How many crayons were not broken?

_____

10

Start with 149. Write backwards to 100.

149				
				100

Writing Numbers: 150 to 199

Start with 199. Write backwards to 150.

199				
				150

Problem Solving

Solve each problem by writing the difference.

1.
$$
\begin{array}{r} 15 \\ -8 \\ \hline \mathbf{7} \end{array} \qquad
\begin{array}{r} 13 \\ -7 \\ \hline \end{array} \qquad
\begin{array}{r} 16 \\ -4 \\ \hline \end{array} \qquad
\begin{array}{r} 18 \\ -18 \\ \hline \end{array} \qquad
\begin{array}{r} 17 \\ -6 \\ \hline \end{array}
$$

2.
$$
\begin{array}{r} 14 \\ -11 \\ \hline \end{array} \qquad
\begin{array}{r} 16 \\ -2 \\ \hline \end{array} \qquad
\begin{array}{r} 15 \\ -15 \\ \hline \end{array} \qquad
\begin{array}{r} 13 \\ -9 \\ \hline \end{array} \qquad
\begin{array}{r} 18 \\ -5 \\ \hline \end{array}
$$

3.
$$
\begin{array}{r} 17 \\ -0 \\ \hline \end{array} \qquad
\begin{array}{r} 16 \\ -10 \\ \hline \end{array} \qquad
\begin{array}{r} 14 \\ -3 \\ \hline \end{array} \qquad
\begin{array}{r} 17 \\ -10 \\ \hline \end{array} \qquad
\begin{array}{r} 16 \\ -0 \\ \hline \end{array}
$$

4.
$$
\begin{array}{r} 14 \\ -7 \\ \hline \end{array} \qquad
\begin{array}{r} 15 \\ -6 \\ \hline \end{array} \qquad
\begin{array}{r} 15 \\ -11 \\ \hline \end{array} \qquad
\begin{array}{r} 12 \\ -10 \\ \hline \end{array} \qquad
\begin{array}{r} 18 \\ -2 \\ \hline \end{array}
$$

Problem Solving

Solve each problem by writing the difference.

1.

16	13	18	14	15
−7	−2	−16	−5	−12
9				

2.

18	14	16	17	14
−1	−9	−3	−8	−10

3.

15	13	18	15	18
−13	−6	−7	−9	−12

4.

13	17	15	14	18
−10	−13	−4	−12	−4

5.

17	15	14	17	12
−11	−15	−6	−2	−4

Matching Equations and Answers

Draw a line to the answer for each problem.

1.

$16 - 12 =$		7
$14 - 7 =$		5
$18 - 17 =$		4
$15 - 10 =$		1
$13 - 11 =$		2

2.

$18 - 3 =$		15
$15 - 7 =$		1
$14 - 4 =$		8
$13 - 12 =$		10
$16 - 8 =$		8

3.

$17 - 4 =$		11
$13 - 3 =$		18
$16 - 5 =$		10
$15 - 14 =$		13
$18 - 0 =$		1

4.

$14 - 13 =$		8
$13 - 4 =$		1
$16 - 9 =$		9
$15 - 3 =$		7
$17 - 9 =$		12

5.

$16 - 1 =$		1
$13 - 8 =$		5
$16 - 15 =$		12
$18 - 6 =$		15
$17 - 7 =$		10

6.

$16 - 11 =$		1
$14 - 13 =$		5
$18 - 8 =$		9
$17 - 8 =$		10
$14 - 1 =$		13

15

Matching Equations and Answers

Draw a line to the answer for each problem.

1.

$18 - 2 =$		13
$13 - 5 =$		8
$15 - 2 =$		9
$16 - 6 =$		10
$18 - 9 =$		16

2.

$14 - 13 =$		2
$16 - 14 =$		10
$18 - 8 =$		4
$18 - 14 =$		0
$13 - 13 =$		1

3.

$16 - 16 =$		12
$15 - 1 =$		13
$17 - 5 =$		14
$18 - 11 =$		0
$13 - 0 =$		7

4.

$18 - 10 =$		8
$13 - 1 =$		4
$17 - 17 =$		12
$15 - 11 =$		13
$16 - 3 =$		0

5.

$17 - 12 =$		3
$13 - 5 =$		5
$18 - 15 =$		9
$16 - 7 =$		8
$18 - 4 =$		14

6.

$18 - 13 =$		12
$13 - 6 =$		8
$16 - 4 =$		4
$14 - 6 =$		7
$15 - 11 =$		5

Problem Solving

Solve each problem below.

1.
$$17 - 11 = 6$$
$$18 - 0$$
$$11 - 4$$
$$7 - 6$$
$$16 - 11$$

2.
$$18 - 4$$
$$11 - 3$$
$$8 - 8$$
$$16 - 9$$
$$14 - 5$$

3.
$$14 - 4$$
$$15 - 12$$
$$9 - 7$$
$$18 - 12$$
$$9 - 6$$

4.
$$17 - 10$$
$$9 - 9$$
$$15 - 0$$
$$16 - 7$$
$$16 - 0$$

5.
$$18 - 6$$
$$15 - 10$$
$$14 - 4$$
$$16 - 6$$
$$12 - 3$$

6.
$$14 - 9$$
$$13 - 5$$
$$15 - 9$$
$$16 - 8$$
$$11 - 2$$

Solve each problem below.

1.
$$15 - 2 = 13$$ $$16 - 5$$ $$14 - 11$$ $$13 - 7$$ $$10 - 7$$

2.
$$12 - 4$$ $$18 - 17$$ $$13 - 6$$ $$12 - 7$$ $$13 - 2$$

3.
$$18 - 11$$ $$13 - 10$$ $$14 - 3$$ $$18 - 0$$ $$17 - 3$$

4.
$$18 - 1$$ $$14 - 14$$ $$12 - 4$$ $$13 - 1$$ $$14 - 7$$

5.
$$14 - 2$$ $$15 - 4$$ $$15 - 7$$ $$13 - 4$$ $$12 - 5$$

Start with 249. Write backwards to 200.

249				
				200

Start with 299. Write backwards to 250.

299				
				250

Word Problem Solving

Read the story. Write the problem and the answer on the lines or in the boxes.

1. The children in room 9 go to school at 9:00. They go to lunch at 12:00. How many hours have they been in school before they go to lunch?

12 – 9 = 3 hours

2. The children get out of school at 3:00. Joe had to leave at 1:00. How much school did he miss?

3. 19 children each had to do a report. 8 children did reports on butter-flies. How many children did not do reports on butter-flies?

4. After recess the children read to themselves. Griffin read 12 pages, and his friend read 9 pages. How many more pages did Griffin read?

Changing Number Words to Numerals

Write the number after the number word.

1.

one	**1**
ten	_____
six	_____
four	_____
nine	_____

2.

five	_____
zero	_____
eleven	_____
seven	_____
two	_____
eight	_____

3.

three	_____
fourteen	_____
thirty	_____
sixteen	_____
fifty	_____

4.

thirty-one	_____
thirteen	_____
forty-three	_____
eighty-nine	_____
twenty-four	_____

5.

seventy-five	_____
twenty-nine	_____
sixty-seven	_____
eighteen	_____
sixty-eight	_____

6.

ninety-nine	_____
fifteen	_____
eighty-eight	_____
one hundred	_____
seventeen	_____

Start with 349. Write backwards to 300.

349				
				300

Start with 399. Write backwards to 350.

399				
				350

Subtracting 2-Digit Numbers

Write the difference. Subtract the ones column first.

ones column
↓

1.
$$\begin{array}{r} 24 \\ -14 \\ \hline \mathbf{10} \end{array}\qquad \begin{array}{r} 64 \\ -24 \\ \hline \end{array}\qquad \begin{array}{r} 83 \\ -32 \\ \hline \end{array}\qquad \begin{array}{r} 46 \\ -15 \\ \hline \end{array}\qquad \begin{array}{r} 87 \\ -32 \\ \hline \end{array}$$

2.
$$\begin{array}{r} 98 \\ -84 \\ \hline \end{array}\qquad \begin{array}{r} 32 \\ -12 \\ \hline \end{array}\qquad \begin{array}{r} 57 \\ -34 \\ \hline \end{array}\qquad \begin{array}{r} 75 \\ -62 \\ \hline \end{array}\qquad \begin{array}{r} 29 \\ -19 \\ \hline \end{array}$$

3.
$$\begin{array}{r} 59 \\ -53 \\ \hline \end{array}\qquad \begin{array}{r} 18 \\ -2 \\ \hline \end{array}\qquad \begin{array}{r} 80 \\ -30 \\ \hline \end{array}\qquad \begin{array}{r} 37 \\ -14 \\ \hline \end{array}\qquad \begin{array}{r} 66 \\ -22 \\ \hline \end{array}$$

4.
$$\begin{array}{r} 16 \\ -6 \\ \hline \end{array}\qquad \begin{array}{r} 88 \\ -44 \\ \hline \end{array}\qquad \begin{array}{r} 99 \\ -35 \\ \hline \end{array}\qquad \begin{array}{r} 48 \\ -26 \\ \hline \end{array}\qquad \begin{array}{r} 62 \\ -12 \\ \hline \end{array}$$

5.
$$\begin{array}{r} 38 \\ -16 \\ \hline \end{array}\qquad \begin{array}{r} 72 \\ -32 \\ \hline \end{array}\qquad \begin{array}{r} 96 \\ -13 \\ \hline \end{array}\qquad \begin{array}{r} 44 \\ -12 \\ \hline \end{array}\qquad \begin{array}{r} 65 \\ -10 \\ \hline \end{array}$$

Subtraction Grade 2—RBP3756

Write the difference. Subtract the ones column first.

ones column

1.
27	72	33	45	39
− 24	− 21	− 20	− 5	− 17
3				

2.
| 39 | 50 | 77 | 81 | 28 |
| − 38 | − 40 | − 25 | − 30 | − 12 |

3.
| 94 | 63 | 36 | 10 | 47 |
| − 82 | − 43 | − 34 | − 5 | − 16 |

4.
| 81 | 25 | 55 | 82 | 69 |
| − 41 | − 24 | − 40 | − 10 | − 24 |

5.
| 75 | 19 | 96 | 73 | 29 |
| − 45 | − 8 | − 33 | − 52 | − 21 |

Subtracting 2-Digit Numbers

Write the difference. Subtract the ones column first.

ones column
↓

1.	78 − 14 **64**	36 − 21	95 − 11	17 − 12	84 − 42
2.	20 − 20	75 − 22	60 − 50	95 − 41	84 − 62
3.	16 − 3	38 − 25	78 − 27	55 − 24	45 − 24
4.	75 − 54	80 − 10	20 − 10	68 − 11	62 − 51
5.	47 − 24	66 − 32	54 − 21	88 − 17	57 − 36

Writing Numbers: 400 to 449

Start with 449. Write backwards to 400.

449				
				400

Start with 499. Write backwards to 450.

499				
				450

Subtracting 3-Digit Numbers

Solve each problem below. Subtract the ones column first, then the tens column. Subtract the hundreds column last.

hundreds ↓ ↓ tens

1.

$$
\begin{array}{r} 864 \\ -123 \\ \hline \mathbf{741} \end{array}
\qquad
\begin{array}{r} 286 \\ -133 \\ \hline \end{array}
\qquad
\begin{array}{r} 648 \\ -141 \\ \hline \end{array}
\qquad
\begin{array}{r} 984 \\ -400 \\ \hline \end{array}
\qquad
\begin{array}{r} 748 \\ -124 \\ \hline \end{array}
$$

2.

$$
\begin{array}{r} 576 \\ -201 \\ \hline \end{array}
\qquad
\begin{array}{r} 698 \\ -568 \\ \hline \end{array}
\qquad
\begin{array}{r} 379 \\ -141 \\ \hline \end{array}
\qquad
\begin{array}{r} 840 \\ -130 \\ \hline \end{array}
\qquad
\begin{array}{r} 695 \\ -645 \\ \hline \end{array}
$$

3.

$$
\begin{array}{r} 127 \\ -13 \\ \hline \end{array}
\qquad
\begin{array}{r} 762 \\ -241 \\ \hline \end{array}
\qquad
\begin{array}{r} 844 \\ -523 \\ \hline \end{array}
\qquad
\begin{array}{r} 539 \\ -425 \\ \hline \end{array}
\qquad
\begin{array}{r} 775 \\ -225 \\ \hline \end{array}
$$

4.

$$
\begin{array}{r} 572 \\ -122 \\ \hline \end{array}
\qquad
\begin{array}{r} 937 \\ -725 \\ \hline \end{array}
\qquad
\begin{array}{r} 623 \\ -102 \\ \hline \end{array}
\qquad
\begin{array}{r} 254 \\ -12 \\ \hline \end{array}
\qquad
\begin{array}{r} 742 \\ -112 \\ \hline \end{array}
$$

5.

$$
\begin{array}{r} 670 \\ -240 \\ \hline \end{array}
\qquad
\begin{array}{r} 938 \\ -526 \\ \hline \end{array}
\qquad
\begin{array}{r} 263 \\ -142 \\ \hline \end{array}
\qquad
\begin{array}{r} 400 \\ -200 \\ \hline \end{array}
\qquad
\begin{array}{r} 624 \\ -512 \\ \hline \end{array}
$$

Subtracting 3-Digit Numbers

Solve each problem below.

1.
$$245 - 124 = \mathbf{121}$$ | $$667 - 324$$ | $$263 - 152$$ | $$314 - 13$$ | $$867 - 120$$

2.
$$678 - 542$$ | $$912 - 801$$ | $$777 - 245$$ | $$309 - 103$$ | $$299 - 46$$

3.
$$286 - 233$$ | $$352 - 230$$ | $$468 - 327$$ | $$258 - 134$$ | $$951 - 900$$

4.
$$486 - 322$$ | $$592 - 371$$ | $$579 - 263$$ | $$368 - 122$$ | $$279 - 100$$

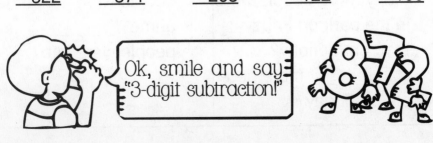

Ok, smile and say "3-digit subtraction!"

31

Subtracting 3-Digit Numbers

Read the story. Write the problem and the answer in the boxes or on the lines below.

1. We went on a trip last summer. The first day we drove 241 miles, and on the second day we drove 452 miles. How many more miles did we drive on the second day?

$$
\begin{array}{r}
452 \\
- 241 \\
\hline
211
\end{array}
$$

_____ miles

2. Ms. Hansen had 567 candles for sale in her store. By the end of the day, she had sold 325. How many candles did she have left?

_____ candles left

3. There were 160 people in the park on Monday. On Friday there were 286. How many more people were in the park on Friday than on Monday?

_____ more people on Friday

4. There were 724 people at the ball game. When it began to rain 510 left. How many people were left at the game? _____ people were left.

Start with 549. Write backwards to 500.

549				
				500

Start with 599. Write backwards to 550.

599				
				550

Start with 649. Write backwards to 600.

649				
				600

Start with 699. Write to 650.

699				
				650

Fractions: Identifying Fractions

Circle the fraction that tells how much is shaded.

1.

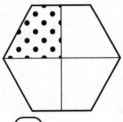

$\frac{1}{2}$ $\boxed{\frac{1}{4}}$ $\frac{1}{3}$ $\frac{2}{4}$

2.

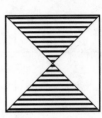

$\frac{2}{4}$ $\frac{3}{4}$ $\frac{1}{8}$ $\frac{1}{4}$

3.

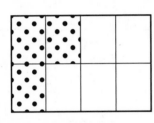

$\frac{3}{8}$ $\frac{5}{8}$ $\frac{1}{4}$ $\frac{5}{9}$

4.

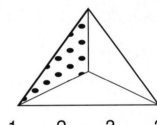

$\frac{1}{3}$ $\frac{2}{3}$ $\frac{3}{3}$ $\frac{2}{12}$

Who's ready for 1/6 of a pizza?

Fractions: Writing Fractions

Write the fraction in the box that tells how much
is **<u>not</u>** shaded.

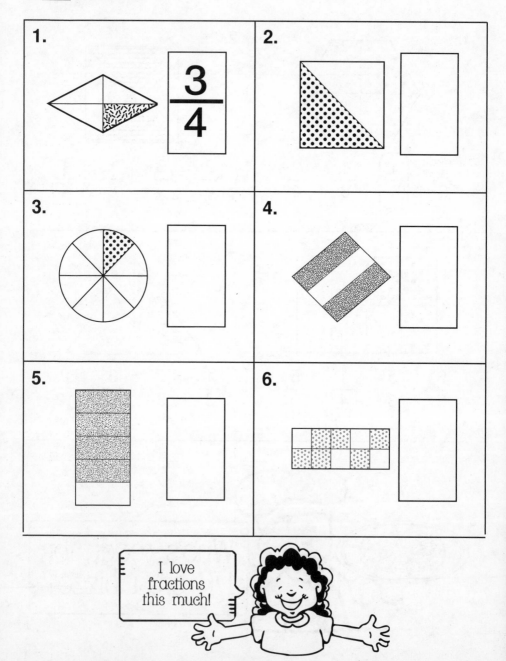

1.

$$\frac{3}{4}$$

2.

3.

4.

5.

6.

I love
fractions
this much!

38

2-Digit Subtraction with Regrouping

Subtract the problems, starting in the ones place. Regroup if you need to.

1. $\overset{2\ 1}{\cancel{3}6}$ 33   51   53   84
    $-\ 17$ $-\ 14$ $-\ 34$ $-\ 24$ $-\ 27$
    19

2. 85   64   67   30   34
    $-\ 26$ $-\ 18$ $-\ 29$ $-\ 18$ $-\ 17$

3. 61   43   20   35   43
    $-\ 32$ $-\ 34$ $-\ 12$ $-\ 16$ $-\ 28$

4. 83   52   63   77   66
    $-\ 55$ $-\ 35$ $-\ 26$ $-\ 38$ $-\ 48$

5. 65   31   52   78   83
    $-\ 17$ $-\ 24$ $-\ 14$ $-\ 29$ $-\ 26$

2-Digit Subtraction with Regrouping

Subtract the problems, starting in the ones place.
Regroup if you need to.

1.
$$\begin{array}{r} \overset{8\ 1}{\cancel{9}6} \\ -\ 28 \\ \hline 68 \end{array}$$
$$\begin{array}{r} 84 \\ -\ 39 \\ \hline \end{array}$$
$$\begin{array}{r} 47 \\ -\ 18 \\ \hline \end{array}$$
$$\begin{array}{r} 64 \\ -\ 47 \\ \hline \end{array}$$
$$\begin{array}{r} 22 \\ -\ 8 \\ \hline \end{array}$$

2.
$$\begin{array}{r} 95 \\ -\ 47 \\ \hline \end{array}$$
$$\begin{array}{r} 14 \\ -\ 9 \\ \hline \end{array}$$
$$\begin{array}{r} 24 \\ -\ 10 \\ \hline \end{array}$$
$$\begin{array}{r} 26 \\ -\ 15 \\ \hline \end{array}$$
$$\begin{array}{r} 31 \\ -\ 17 \\ \hline \end{array}$$

3.
$$\begin{array}{r} 62 \\ -\ 36 \\ \hline \end{array}$$
$$\begin{array}{r} 85 \\ -\ 46 \\ \hline \end{array}$$
$$\begin{array}{r} 74 \\ -\ 28 \\ \hline \end{array}$$
$$\begin{array}{r} 72 \\ -\ 8 \\ \hline \end{array}$$
$$\begin{array}{r} 80 \\ -\ 18 \\ \hline \end{array}$$

4.
$$\begin{array}{r} 75 \\ -\ 38 \\ \hline \end{array}$$
$$\begin{array}{r} 16 \\ -\ 9 \\ \hline \end{array}$$
$$\begin{array}{r} 65 \\ -\ 16 \\ \hline \end{array}$$
$$\begin{array}{r} 18 \\ -\ 9 \\ \hline \end{array}$$
$$\begin{array}{r} 42 \\ -\ 28 \\ \hline \end{array}$$

5.
$$\begin{array}{r} 51 \\ -\ 42 \\ \hline \end{array}$$
$$\begin{array}{r} 45 \\ -\ 26 \\ \hline \end{array}$$
$$\begin{array}{r} 71 \\ -\ 12 \\ \hline \end{array}$$
$$\begin{array}{r} 82 \\ -\ 16 \\ \hline \end{array}$$
$$\begin{array}{r} 48 \\ -\ 16 \\ \hline \end{array}$$

2-Digit Subtraction with Regrouping

Subtract the problems, starting in the ones place.
Regroup if you need to.

1.
$$\begin{array}{r} {}^{5}\cancel{6}{}^{1}1 \\ -\ 33 \\ \hline \mathbf{28} \end{array}$$
$$\begin{array}{r} 50 \\ -13 \\ \hline \end{array}$$
$$\begin{array}{r} 62 \\ -\ 3 \\ \hline \end{array}$$
$$\begin{array}{r} 72 \\ -14 \\ \hline \end{array}$$
$$\begin{array}{r} 31 \\ -18 \\ \hline \end{array}$$

2.
$$\begin{array}{r} 47 \\ -29 \\ \hline \end{array}$$
$$\begin{array}{r} 43 \\ -31 \\ \hline \end{array}$$
$$\begin{array}{r} 71 \\ -35 \\ \hline \end{array}$$
$$\begin{array}{r} 90 \\ -55 \\ \hline \end{array}$$
$$\begin{array}{r} 61 \\ -19 \\ \hline \end{array}$$

3.
$$\begin{array}{r} 58 \\ -29 \\ \hline \end{array}$$
$$\begin{array}{r} 32 \\ -13 \\ \hline \end{array}$$
$$\begin{array}{r} 82 \\ -36 \\ \hline \end{array}$$
$$\begin{array}{r} 81 \\ -28 \\ \hline \end{array}$$
$$\begin{array}{r} 33 \\ -15 \\ \hline \end{array}$$

4.
$$\begin{array}{r} 50 \\ -35 \\ \hline \end{array}$$
$$\begin{array}{r} 77 \\ -39 \\ \hline \end{array}$$
$$\begin{array}{r} 91 \\ -34 \\ \hline \end{array}$$
$$\begin{array}{r} 20 \\ -\ 2 \\ \hline \end{array}$$
$$\begin{array}{r} 72 \\ -\ 4 \\ \hline \end{array}$$

5.
$$\begin{array}{r} 26 \\ -18 \\ \hline \end{array}$$
$$\begin{array}{r} 53 \\ -36 \\ \hline \end{array}$$
$$\begin{array}{r} 42 \\ -37 \\ \hline \end{array}$$
$$\begin{array}{r} 44 \\ -25 \\ \hline \end{array}$$
$$\begin{array}{r} 27 \\ -\ 4 \\ \hline \end{array}$$

2-Digit Subtraction with Some Regrouping

Subtract. Regroup if you need to.

1.
$$\begin{array}{r} \overset{2}{\cancel{3}}\overset{1}{4} \\ -\ 18 \\ \hline \mathbf{16} \end{array}$$
$$\begin{array}{r} 51 \\ -\ 38 \\ \hline \end{array}$$
$$\begin{array}{r} 42 \\ -\ 16 \\ \hline \end{array}$$
$$\begin{array}{r} 38 \\ -\ 22 \\ \hline \end{array}$$
$$\begin{array}{r} 49 \\ -\ 28 \\ \hline \end{array}$$

2.
$$\begin{array}{r} 25 \\ -\ 13 \\ \hline \end{array}$$
$$\begin{array}{r} 30 \\ -\ 19 \\ \hline \end{array}$$
$$\begin{array}{r} 56 \\ -\ 42 \\ \hline \end{array}$$
$$\begin{array}{r} 83 \\ -\ 38 \\ \hline \end{array}$$
$$\begin{array}{r} 77 \\ -\ 44 \\ \hline \end{array}$$

3.
$$\begin{array}{r} 16 \\ -\ 8 \\ \hline \end{array}$$
$$\begin{array}{r} 33 \\ -\ 30 \\ \hline \end{array}$$
$$\begin{array}{r} 88 \\ -\ 38 \\ \hline \end{array}$$
$$\begin{array}{r} 64 \\ -\ 25 \\ \hline \end{array}$$
$$\begin{array}{r} 23 \\ -\ 20 \\ \hline \end{array}$$

4.
$$\begin{array}{r} 44 \\ -\ 26 \\ \hline \end{array}$$
$$\begin{array}{r} 75 \\ -\ 67 \\ \hline \end{array}$$
$$\begin{array}{r} 23 \\ -\ 13 \\ \hline \end{array}$$
$$\begin{array}{r} 67 \\ -\ 39 \\ \hline \end{array}$$
$$\begin{array}{r} 84 \\ -\ 15 \\ \hline \end{array}$$

5.
$$\begin{array}{r} 63 \\ -\ 47 \\ \hline \end{array}$$
$$\begin{array}{r} 24 \\ -\ 14 \\ \hline \end{array}$$
$$\begin{array}{r} 27 \\ -\ 9 \\ \hline \end{array}$$
$$\begin{array}{r} 76 \\ -\ 17 \\ \hline \end{array}$$
$$\begin{array}{r} 54 \\ -\ 18 \\ \hline \end{array}$$

2-Digit Subtraction with Some Regrouping

Subtract. Regroup if you need to.

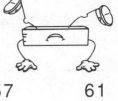

1. $\begin{array}{r} 48 \\ -28 \\ \hline \mathbf{20} \end{array}$ $\begin{array}{r} 32 \\ -13 \\ \hline \end{array}$ $\begin{array}{r} 16 \\ -9 \\ \hline \end{array}$ $\begin{array}{r} 57 \\ -45 \\ \hline \end{array}$ $\begin{array}{r} 61 \\ -28 \\ \hline \end{array}$

2. $\begin{array}{r} 95 \\ -27 \\ \hline \end{array}$ $\begin{array}{r} 67 \\ -27 \\ \hline \end{array}$ $\begin{array}{r} 47 \\ -19 \\ \hline \end{array}$ $\begin{array}{r} 51 \\ -33 \\ \hline \end{array}$ $\begin{array}{r} 93 \\ -46 \\ \hline \end{array}$

3. $\begin{array}{r} 24 \\ -15 \\ \hline \end{array}$ $\begin{array}{r} 60 \\ -37 \\ \hline \end{array}$ $\begin{array}{r} 36 \\ -13 \\ \hline \end{array}$ $\begin{array}{r} 57 \\ -28 \\ \hline \end{array}$ $\begin{array}{r} 25 \\ -15 \\ \hline \end{array}$

4. $\begin{array}{r} 60 \\ -42 \\ \hline \end{array}$ $\begin{array}{r} 88 \\ -46 \\ \hline \end{array}$ $\begin{array}{r} 65 \\ -48 \\ \hline \end{array}$ $\begin{array}{r} 46 \\ -32 \\ \hline \end{array}$ $\begin{array}{r} 21 \\ -15 \\ \hline \end{array}$

5. $\begin{array}{r} 55 \\ -15 \\ \hline \end{array}$ $\begin{array}{r} 67 \\ -27 \\ \hline \end{array}$ $\begin{array}{r} 82 \\ -16 \\ \hline \end{array}$ $\begin{array}{r} 48 \\ -17 \\ \hline \end{array}$ $\begin{array}{r} 22 \\ -17 \\ \hline \end{array}$

Problem Solving

Subtract and write the answers on the lines. Circle the problems in each box that have the same answer.

1.

$24 - 12 = \underline{\textbf{12}}$

$39 - 27 = \underline{}$

$16 - 12 = \underline{}$

$47 - 44 = \underline{}$

$50 - 38 = \underline{}$

$22 - 11 = \underline{}$

2.

$67 - 29 = \underline{}$

$21 - 9 = \underline{}$

$43 - 26 = \underline{}$

$55 - 38 = \underline{}$

$72 - 14 = \underline{}$

$33 - 16 = \underline{}$

3.

$42 - 16 = \underline{}$

$94 - 68 = \underline{}$

$32 - 14 = \underline{}$

$17 - 16 = \underline{}$

$87 - 61 = \underline{}$

$36 - 10 = \underline{}$

4.

$44 - 19 = \underline{}$

$32 - 11 = \underline{}$

$61 - 31 = \underline{}$

$24 - 22 = \underline{}$

$55 - 25 = \underline{}$

$48 - 18 = \underline{}$

Word Problem Solving

Read the story. Write the problem and answer in the boxes.

1. We put 42 cans of fruit on the shelf. A lady bought 14 of them. How many cans are left on the shelf?

42
– 14
28

2. Denise's box of animal crackers had 41 crackers. Matt's box had 67. How many more did Matt have?

3. I lined up 52 dominoes. 14 of them did not fall over. How many dominoes **did** fall?

4. Lori is going on a trip for 21 days this year. Last year she went for 18 days. How many more days will she be on her trip this year than last year?

Word Problem Solving

Read the story. Write the problem and answer in the boxes.

1. We counted 84 peaches on our tree. Some fell off. There are still 68 on the tree. How many fell off?

$$84$$
$$-\ 68$$
$$16$$

2. My friend and I tried to guess how many jelly beans were in a bag at the store. I guessed 48; my friend guessed 97. How many more did she guess?

3. Allie collected 78 bottle caps. Rob collected 29 fewer than Allie. How many did Rob collect?

4. After school on Tuesday, 86 children went swimming. 19 of them left before the others. How many were still at the pool?

Problem Solving

Subtract and write the answers on the lines. Circle the problems in each box that have the same answer.

1.

54 − 19 = _____

51 − 38 = _____

62 − 30 = _____

43 − 26 = _____

26 − 13 = _____

44 − 40 = _____

2.

75 − 33 = _____

71 − 23 = _____

90 − 50 = _____

77 − 57 = _____

38 − 24 = _____

87 − 45 = _____

3.

15 − 12 = _____

59 − 56 = _____

21 − 18 = _____

38 − 35 = _____

45 − 42 = _____

18 − 9 = _____

4.

94 − 18 = _____

49 − 24 = _____

38 − 13 = _____

82 − 47 = _____

52 − 27 = _____

67 − 42 = _____

I'm sure you'll have no problem finishing these problems!

© BBB Books   Subtraction Grade 2—BBP3756

3-Digit Subtraction with Regrouping

Subtract the problems, starting in the ones place. Regroup if you need to.

1.
$$
\begin{array}{r} \overset{5\ 11\ 1}{6\cancel{2}4} \\ -\ 135 \\ \hline 489 \end{array}
\qquad
\begin{array}{r} 162 \\ -\ 13 \\ \hline \end{array}
\qquad
\begin{array}{r} 609 \\ -\ 319 \\ \hline \end{array}
\qquad
\begin{array}{r} 378 \\ -\ 179 \\ \hline \end{array}
\qquad
\begin{array}{r} 809 \\ -\ 512 \\ \hline \end{array}
$$

2.
$$
\begin{array}{r} 564 \\ -\ 377 \\ \hline \end{array}
\qquad
\begin{array}{r} 850 \\ -\ 8 \\ \hline \end{array}
\qquad
\begin{array}{r} 269 \\ -\ 94 \\ \hline \end{array}
\qquad
\begin{array}{r} 460 \\ -\ 278 \\ \hline \end{array}
\qquad
\begin{array}{r} 648 \\ -\ 129 \\ \hline \end{array}
$$

3.
$$
\begin{array}{r} 528 \\ -\ 134 \\ \hline \end{array}
\qquad
\begin{array}{r} 437 \\ -\ 129 \\ \hline \end{array}
\qquad
\begin{array}{r} 644 \\ -\ 246 \\ \hline \end{array}
\qquad
\begin{array}{r} 434 \\ -\ 225 \\ \hline \end{array}
\qquad
\begin{array}{r} 942 \\ -\ 367 \\ \hline \end{array}
$$

4.
$$
\begin{array}{r} 410 \\ -\ 132 \\ \hline \end{array}
\qquad
\begin{array}{r} 840 \\ -\ 38 \\ \hline \end{array}
\qquad
\begin{array}{r} 864 \\ -\ 239 \\ \hline \end{array}
\qquad
\begin{array}{r} 717 \\ -\ 226 \\ \hline \end{array}
\qquad
\begin{array}{r} 547 \\ -\ 139 \\ \hline \end{array}
$$

5.
$$
\begin{array}{r} 236 \\ -\ 129 \\ \hline \end{array}
\qquad
\begin{array}{r} 133 \\ -\ 24 \\ \hline \end{array}
\qquad
\begin{array}{r} 519 \\ -\ 287 \\ \hline \end{array}
\qquad
\begin{array}{r} 933 \\ -\ 100 \\ \hline \end{array}
\qquad
\begin{array}{r} 296 \\ -\ 137 \\ \hline \end{array}
$$

3-Digit Subtraction with Regrouping

Subtract the problems, starting in the ones place. Regroup if you need to.

1.
$$\begin{array}{r} 8\overset{6\;1}{\cancel{7}}5 \\ -\ 406 \\ \hline \mathbf{469} \end{array}$$
  $\begin{array}{r} 141 \\ -\ 57 \\ \hline \end{array}$
  $\begin{array}{r} 843 \\ -\ 327 \\ \hline \end{array}$
  $\begin{array}{r} 648 \\ -\ 252 \\ \hline \end{array}$
  $\begin{array}{r} 286 \\ -\ 137 \\ \hline \end{array}$

2.
$\begin{array}{r} 984 \\ -\ 296 \\ \hline \end{array}$
  $\begin{array}{r} 885 \\ -\ 147 \\ \hline \end{array}$
  $\begin{array}{r} 671 \\ -\ 366 \\ \hline \end{array}$
  $\begin{array}{r} 352 \\ -\ 204 \\ \hline \end{array}$
  $\begin{array}{r} 622 \\ -\ 144 \\ \hline \end{array}$

3.
$\begin{array}{r} 142 \\ -\ 36 \\ \hline \end{array}$
  $\begin{array}{r} 328 \\ -\ 182 \\ \hline \end{array}$
  $\begin{array}{r} 555 \\ -\ 388 \\ \hline \end{array}$
  $\begin{array}{r} 210 \\ -\ 97 \\ \hline \end{array}$
  $\begin{array}{r} 332 \\ -\ 146 \\ \hline \end{array}$

4.
$\begin{array}{r} 300 \\ -\ 132 \\ \hline \end{array}$
  $\begin{array}{r} 379 \\ -\ 289 \\ \hline \end{array}$
  $\begin{array}{r} 521 \\ -\ 139 \\ \hline \end{array}$
  $\begin{array}{r} 110 \\ -\ 79 \\ \hline \end{array}$
  $\begin{array}{r} 213 \\ -\ 142 \\ \hline \end{array}$

5.
$\begin{array}{r} 216 \\ -\ 139 \\ \hline \end{array}$
  $\begin{array}{r} 777 \\ -\ 532 \\ \hline \end{array}$
  $\begin{array}{r} 824 \\ -\ 57 \\ \hline \end{array}$
  $\begin{array}{r} 319 \\ -\ 216 \\ \hline \end{array}$
  $\begin{array}{r} 469 \\ -\ 122 \\ \hline \end{array}$

3-Digit Subtraction with Some Regrouping

Subtract the problems, starting in the ones place. Regroup if you need to.

1.
$$
\begin{array}{r} \overset{5\ 1}{16\cancel{8}} \\ -\ 29 \\ \hline \mathbf{139} \end{array}
\qquad
\begin{array}{r} 422 \\ -\ 145 \\ \hline \end{array}
\qquad
\begin{array}{r} 122 \\ -\ 12 \\ \hline \end{array}
\qquad
\begin{array}{r} 325 \\ -\ 132 \\ \hline \end{array}
\qquad
\begin{array}{r} 745 \\ -\ 146 \\ \hline \end{array}
$$

2.
$$
\begin{array}{r} 109 \\ -\ 98 \\ \hline \end{array}
\qquad
\begin{array}{r} 229 \\ -\ 149 \\ \hline \end{array}
\qquad
\begin{array}{r} 670 \\ -\ 384 \\ \hline \end{array}
\qquad
\begin{array}{r} 639 \\ -\ 327 \\ \hline \end{array}
\qquad
\begin{array}{r} 129 \\ -\ 30 \\ \hline \end{array}
$$

3.
$$
\begin{array}{r} 243 \\ -\ 138 \\ \hline \end{array}
\qquad
\begin{array}{r} 111 \\ -\ 62 \\ \hline \end{array}
\qquad
\begin{array}{r} 775 \\ -\ 187 \\ \hline \end{array}
\qquad
\begin{array}{r} 622 \\ -\ 219 \\ \hline \end{array}
\qquad
\begin{array}{r} 330 \\ -\ 129 \\ \hline \end{array}
$$

4.
$$
\begin{array}{r} 148 \\ -\ 48 \\ \hline \end{array}
\qquad
\begin{array}{r} 394 \\ -\ 139 \\ \hline \end{array}
\qquad
\begin{array}{r} 227 \\ -\ 72 \\ \hline \end{array}
\qquad
\begin{array}{r} 136 \\ -\ 134 \\ \hline \end{array}
\qquad
\begin{array}{r} 296 \\ -\ 98 \\ \hline \end{array}
$$

5.
$$
\begin{array}{r} 480 \\ -\ 246 \\ \hline \end{array}
\qquad
\begin{array}{r} 147 \\ -\ 64 \\ \hline \end{array}
\qquad
\begin{array}{r} 336 \\ -\ 136 \\ \hline \end{array}
\qquad
\begin{array}{r} 126 \\ -\ 113 \\ \hline \end{array}
\qquad
\begin{array}{r} 648 \\ -\ 154 \\ \hline \end{array}
$$

Math Investigations

Principal Johnson gives pencils to children who are "caught being good." He keeps track of how many he gives out so he can get more when needed. He starts with 1,000 pencils. Every hour he checks his supply.

Each picture of a pencil on the chart represents 100 pencils. Write your answers in numbers.

Time	Pencils Given Away	Pencils Re-Stocked	Pencils in Stock
1. 9:00 a.m.	none	none	1,000
2. 10:00 a.m.	🖊🖊🖊🖊	none	
3. 11:00 a.m.	🖊🖊	none	
4. 12:00 p.m.	🖊🖊🖊	🖊🖊🖊🖊	
5. 1:00 p.m.	🖊	🖊🖊	
6. 2:00 p.m.	🖊🖊🖊🖊🖊	🖊🖊🖊🖊🖊	
7. 3:00 p.m.	🖊🖊🖊	none	
8. 4:00 p.m.	🖊	🖊🖊🖊🖊🖊🖊	

How many pencils did Principal Johnson give away?_____

51

Math Investigations

Write a subtraction number sentence for each picture.

$$5 - 3 = 2$$

Now draw your own subtraction picture and write your own number sentence.

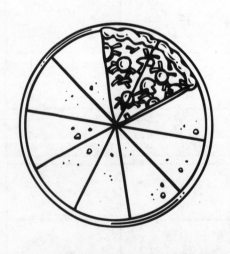

Math Investigations

Sam had 4 dogs.
He gave each dog 15 bones.
Some of the dogs lost their bones.
Write the answers.

		Lost on Day 1	Lost on Day 2	How many are left?
a		🦴🦴	🦴🦴🦴	**10**
b		🦴	🦴🦴 🦴🦴	
c		🦴	🦴🦴🦴 🦴🦴	
d		🦴	🦴	

1. Who lost the most bones on Day 1?_____
2. Who lost the most bones on Day 2?_____
3. Who lost the fewest bones on Day 1?_____
4. Who lost the fewest bones on Day 2?_____
5. Who lost the most bones in all?_____
6. Who lost the fewest bones in all?_____

Math Investigations

Fill in the missing numbers on the chart.

Number	+1	+2	+3	+4	+5
2	3	4	←⑤		
3	4	⑤			
4	⑤		7		9
⑤				9	10

Use the chart to subtract.

5 – 3 = __**2**__
Circle the 5s.
Underline the 5 under
+3. What number is
furthest to the left in that
row?__**2**__

2. 9 – 5 = _____
Circle the 9s in yellow.
Underline the 9 under
+5. What number is the
furthest to the left in the
row?_____

3. 8 – 4 = _____
Circle the 8s in purple.
Underline the 8 under
+4. What number is the
furthest to the left in the
row?_____

Math Investigations

Each elephant had a bag of 12 peanuts.
As they walked home, they ate peanuts.
Follow their paths. Write how many
peanuts each elephant had when he got home. Put a
square around the elephant with the least.

a

b

55

Math Investigations

Matt went fishing. Draw more worms in his bucket. He put a new worm on the hook every time he cast. How many times did he cast if he has 4 worms left?

_____ times

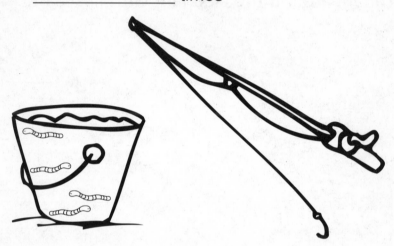

A bea was looking for food. Draw some fish in the river.
The be ir ate 2 fish every day for 4 days.
How m ny fish are left in the river? _____
Did he ave enough fish in the river for all 4 days?_____

Math Investigations

Draw some . Now cross out some to show subtraction. Write the number sentence below. Write how many inside each circle. Write − or = in each square.

Draw some . Now cross out some to show subtraction. Write the number sentence below. Write how many inside each circle. Write − or = in each square.

Draw some  . Now cross out some  to show subtraction. Write the number sentence below. Write how many inside each circle. Write − or = in each square.

Math Investigations

What numbers are missing?

Write the numbers in each ☐.
Subtract across and down.

1.

| 5 ⇨ 2 ⇨ 3 |
| 4 ⇨ 2 ⇨ 2 |
| ⇩   ⇩   ⇩ |
| 1 ⇨ 0 ⇨ 1 |

2.

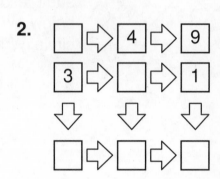

☐ ⇨ 4 ⇨ 9
3 ⇨ ☐ ⇨ 1
⇩ ⇩ ⇩
☐ ⇨ ☐ ⇨ ☐

3.

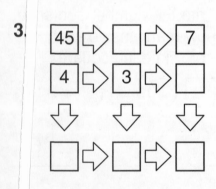

45 ⇨ ☐ ⇨ 7
4 ⇨ 3 ⇨ ☐
⇩ ⇩ ⇩
☐ ⇨ ☐ ⇨ ☐

4.

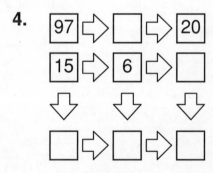

97 ⇨ ☐ ⇨ 20
15 ⇨ 6 ⇨ ☐
⇩ ⇩ ⇩
☐ ⇨ ☐ ⇨ ☐

Math Investigations

Each row follows a rule in subtraction. Write in the missing numbers. Write the rule.

| 100 | 90 | 80 | ___ | ___ | ___ |

100	90	80	70		
− 10	− 10	− 10	− 10	−	−
90	80	70			

RULE: _____

| 100 | 91 | 82 | ___ | ___ | ___ |

100	91	82	73		
− 9	− 9	− 9	− 9	−	−
91	82	73			

RULE: _____

| 100 | 92 | 84 | ___ | ___ | ___ |

100	92	84	76		
− 8	− 8	− 8	− 8	−	−
92	84	76			

RULE: _____

Math Investigations

If you need to regroup 1 ten as 10 ones to solve the problem, color the square green. If you don't need to regroup, do not color the square. The colored squares will show you a face.

29 - 20	62 - 22	73 - 30	69 - 21	44 - 10	34 - 12	83 - 41
36 - 15	41 - 11	50 - 4	79 - 53	20 - 19	82 - 31	94 - 50
45 - 25	67 - 17	75 - 35	69 - 37	96 - 24	41 - 10	82 - 41
29 - 20	62 - 20	73 - 40	70 - 35	44 - 14	34 - 12	83 - 41
38 - 15	41 - 19	50 - 40	75 - 51	30 - 10	80 - 31	94 - 50
95 - 24	77 - 17	75 - 39	60 - 35	56 - 29	31 - 10	72 - 41

Math Investigations

Which rule do the numbers on the animals
follow? Fill in the numbers. Write the rule.

Rule: 18 has been subtracted from each number.

Rule: _____

Rule: _____

Rule: _____

Rule: _____

Math Investigations

You have $2.00 to spend on your vacation. Choose the roads where you will go. Don't overspend, or back home you go!

Draw a line showing the roads you take. Subtract the money you pass on the way to your vacation spot.

Math Investigations

Help the alligator get to the swamp.
Find the nearest ten for each number.
Then follow the path that shows the
estimated difference.

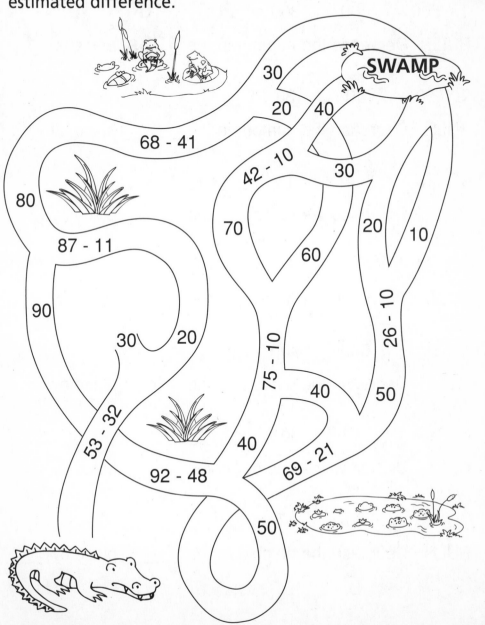

SWAMP

30

20   40

68 - 41

42 - 10   30

80

70   20   10

87 - 11   60

90   26 - 10

30   20

75 - 10

53 - 32   40   50

40

92 - 48   69 - 21

50

63

Math Investigations

What are the next three numbers in each pattern? Complete the rule.

1. 500   400   300   **200   100   0**

RULE: Decrease the number in the **100s** place by **1** .

2. 50   40   30   _____   _____   _____

RULE: Decrease the number in the _____ place by ___ .

3. 15   14   13   _____   _____   _____

RULE: Decrease the number in the _____ place by ___ .

4. 34   32   30   _____   _____   _____

RULE: Decrease the number in the _____ place by ___ .

5. 800   600   400   _____   _____

RULE: Decrease the number in the _____ place by ___ .

6. 501   401   301   _____   _____   _____

RULE: Decrease the number in the _____ place by ___ .

7. 95   90   85   _____   _____   _____

RULE: Decrease the number in the _____ place by ___ .

Greater Than or Less Than

Put the greater than (>) or less than (<) sign in the boxes to complete the problems.

1. 14 ☐ 19   16 ☐ 17   12 ☐ 8   17 ☐ 18

2. 10 ☐ 9   11 ☐ 6   0 ☐ 1   15 ☐ 7

      This bag has black and white marbles in it. Look closely at the marbles. If you could reach in the bag and take out a handful, do you think you would have more black or more white marbles? _____

Why? _____

_____

_____

Brain Teasers

Connect the dots. Count by 5s backwards. Start at 100 and end at zero!

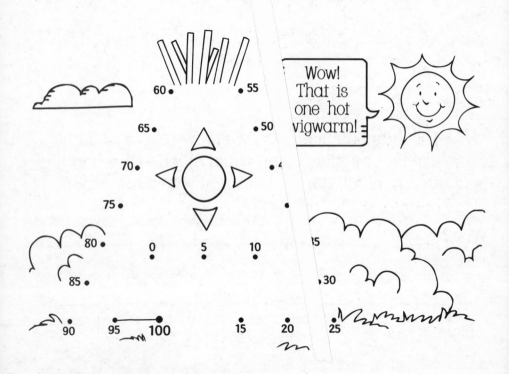

Wow! That is one hot wigwarm!

BRain Teasers

Lori, Denise, and Matt went to the pet store. They each had $5.00 to spend. Lori bought 2 goldfish. Denise bought a puppy. Matt bought a kitten. Use the cost of each animal to decide who had the most money left over.

puppies $2.50 each

kittens $3.00 each

fish $1.00 each

Color the animals that did not get bought.

FACTOID!

There are three states in America that do NOT change their clocks during Daylight Savings Time. Can you guess which ones they are?

Answer: Parts of Indiana, Arizona, and Hawaii are always on Standard Daylight Time.

67

Brain 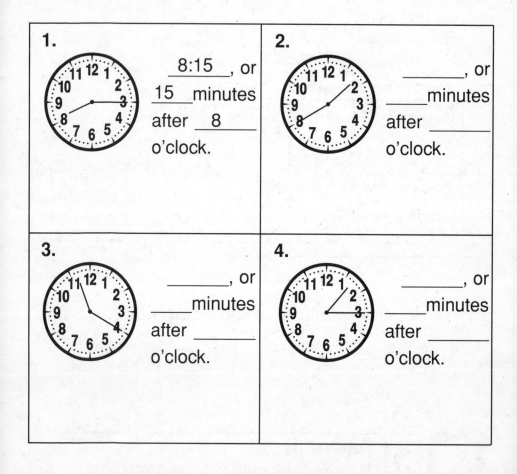 Teasers

Write the time shown on these clocks.
Fill in each blank.

1.

_____8:15_____, or
__15__ minutes
after ___8___
o'clock.

2.

_____, or
_____ minutes
after _____
o'clock.

3.

_____, or
_____ minutes
after _____
o'clock.

4.

_____, or
_____ minutes
after _____
o'clock.

Brain 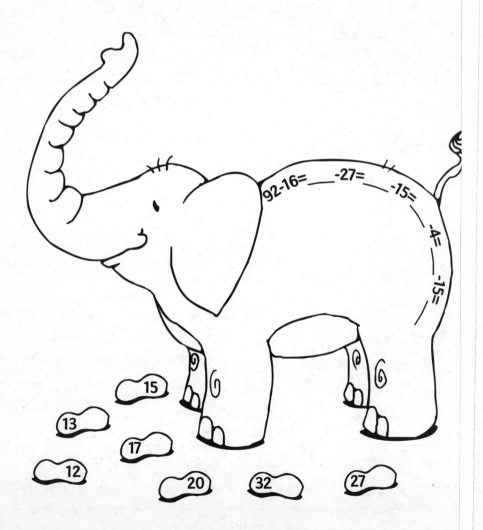 Teasers

How many peanuts did the elephant eat? Solve the equations below to find your answer. Circle the peanut with the correct answer.

92-16=___ -27=___ -15=___ -4=___ -15=___

15

13

17

12

20   32   27

Complete the puzzle on the next page.

Across

1. 17 − 14 = _____

2. Kids go to _____ to learn.

3. This book is about

    _____.

4. 5 − 3 is called an

    _____.

5. 56 − 47 = _____

6. To find the answer is to

    _____ the equation.

Down

1. You have _____ eyes.

2. The number of months in a year minus one.

    _____

3. Something that tells time.

    _____

4. 9 is an odd _____.

5. 27 − 11 = _____

6. The _____ on a clock tell you what time it is.

Word Bank					
three	school	subtraction	equation	nine	solve
clock	eleven	sixteen	number	two	hands

Brain  Teasers

Complete the puzzle using the clues on the previous page.

Factoid!

Question:
You have more than 100,000 hairs on your head. How many hairs do you lose each day?

Answer: 50 to 100 hairs per day.

Subtraction Grade 2 · PRP3756

Brain  Teasers

Solve each equation. Circle the kernels with a difference of an odd number.

1. 59
    − 17

2.
7 − 2 = ___

3. 26
    − 4

popcorn

4. 16
    − 7

5. 67
    − 7

6. 59
    − 13

7. 12
    − 12

8.
89 − 9 = ___

9.
47 − 13 = ___

10.
27 − 13 = ___

Factoid!

American colonists used to make "cereal" by pouring cream over popcorn and serving it for breakfast.

72

www.summerbridgeactivities.com

Answer Pages

Page 3
1. 9, 0, 6, 3, 6
2. 1, 11, 1, 3, 6
3. 10, 2, 5, 3, 6
4. 4, 9, 1, 1, 5
5. 12, 4, 0, 0 , 3

Page 4
1. 8, 5, 3, 0, 8
2. 0, 1, 7, 2, 0
3. 6, 4, 8, 2, 1
4. 6, 4, 5, 3, 3
5. 2, 7, 4, 9, 2

Page 5
1. 10, 4, 8, 8, 2, 3
2. 6, 3, 3, 0, 1, 5
3. 2, 1, 0, 4, 7, 7
4. 6, 3, 0, 10, 0, 2

Page 6
1. 10, 2, 5, 7, 0, 9
2. 3, 7, 1, 11, 5, 7
3. 0, 1, 9, 4, 4, 7
4. 2, 7, 4, 0, 7, 1

Page 7

49	48	47	46	45	44	43	42	41	40
39	38	37	36	35	34	33	32	31	30
29	28	27	26	25	24	23	22	21	20
19	18	17	16	15	14	13	12	11	10
9	8	7	6	5	4	3	2	1	0

1. 46
2. 10
3. 28
4. 33

Page 8

99	98	97	96	95	94	93	92	91	90
89	88	87	86	85	84	83	82	81	80
79	78	77	76	75	74	73	72	71	70
69	68	67	66	65	64	63	62	61	60
59	58	57	56	55	54	53	52	51	50

1. 52, 54, 56, 58
2. 83, 85, 87, 89
3. 66

Page 9
1. 3, 7, 2, 0, 1
2. 3, 7, 7, 4, 3
3. 2, 0, 3, 6, 8
4. 4, 0, 4, 6, 11
5. 3, 4, 4, 4, 8

Page 10
1. $9 - 7 = 2$
2. $5 - 3 = 2$
3. $10 - 7 = 3$
4. $12 - 6 = 6$

Page 11

149	148	147	146	145	144	143	142	141	140
139	138	137	136	135	134	133	132	131	130
129	128	127	126	125	124	123	122	121	120
119	118	117	116	115	114	113	112	111	110
109	108	107	106	105	104	103	102	101	100

Page 12

199	198	197	196	195	194	193	192	191	190
189	188	187	186	185	184	183	182	181	180
179	178	177	176	175	174	173	172	171	170
169	168	167	166	165	164	163	162	161	160
159	158	157	156	155	154	153	152	151	150

Answer Pages

Page 13
1. 7, 6, 12, 0, 11
2. 3, 14, 0, 4, 13
3. 17, 6, 11, 7, 16
4. 7, 9, 4, 2, 16

Page 14
1. 9, 11, 2, 9, 3
2. 17, 5, 13, 9, 4
3. 2, 7, 11, 6, 6
4. 3, 4, 11, 2, 14
5. 6, 0, 8, 15, 8

Page 15

1.
16 - 12 = 7
14 - 7 = 5
18 - 17 = 4
15 - 10 = 1
13 - 11 = 2

2.
18 - 3 = 15
15 - 7 = 1
14 - 4 = 8
13 - 12 = 10
16 - 8 = 8

3.
17 - 4 = 11
13 - 3 = 18
16 - 5 = 10
15 - 14 = 13
18 - 0 = 1

4.
14 - 13 = 8
13 - 4 = 1
16 - 9 = 9
15 - 3 = 7
17 - 9 = 12

5.
16 - 1 = 1
13 - 8 = 5
16 - 15 = 12
18 - 6 = 15
17 - 7 = 10

6.
16 - 11 = 1
14 - 13 = 5
18 - 8 = 9
17 - 8 = 10
14 - 1 = 13

Page 16

1.
18 - = 13
13 - = 8
15 - = 9
16 - = 10
18 - 9 = 16

2.
14 - 13 = 2
16 - 14 = 10
18 - 8 = 4
18 - 14 = 0
13 - 13 = 1

3.
16 - 16 = 12
15 - 1 = 13
17 - 5 = 14
18 - 11 = 0
13 - 0 = 7

4.
18 - 10 = 8
13 - 1 = 4
17 - 17 = 12
15 - 11 = 13
16 - 3 = 0

5.
17 - 12 = 3
13 - 5 = 5
18 - 15 = 9
16 - 7 = 8
18 - 4 = 14

6.
18 - 13 = 12
13 - 6 = 8
16 - 4 = 4
14 - 6 = 7
15 - 11 = 5

Page 17
1. 6, 18, 7, 1, 5
2. 14, 8, 0, 7, 9
3. 10, 3, 2, 6, 3
4. 7, 0, 15, 9, 16
5. 12, 5, 10, 10, 9
6. 5, 8, 6, 8, 9

Page 18
1. 13, 11, 3, 6, 3
2. 8, 1, 7, 5, 11
3. 7, 3, 11, 18, 14
4. 17, 0, 8, 12, 7
5. 12, 11, 8, 9, 7

Page 19

249	248	247	246	245	244	243	242	241	240
239	238	237	236	235	234	233	232	231	230
229	228	227	226	225	224	223	222	221	220
219	218	217	216	215	214	213	212	211	210
209	208	207	206	205	204	203	202	201	200

Page 20

299	298	297	296	295	294	293	292	291	290
289	288	287	286	285	284	283	282	281	280
279	278	277	276	275	274	273	272	271	270
269	268	267	266	265	264	263	262	261	260
259	258	257	256	255	254	253	252	251	250

Page 21
1. 3 hours
2. 2 hours
3. 8 children
4. 3 pages

Answer Pages

Page 22
1. 1, 10, 6, 4, 9
2. 5, 0, 11, 7, 2, 8
3. 3, 14, 30, 16, 50
4. 31, 13, 43, 89, 24
5. 75, 29, 67, 18, 68
6. 99, 15, 88, 100, 17

Page 23

349	348	347	346	345	344	343	342	341	340
339	338	337	336	335	334	333	332	331	330
329	328	327	326	325	324	323	322	321	320
319	318	317	316	315	314	313	312	311	310
309	308	307	306	305	304	303	302	301	300

Page 24

399	398	397	396	395	394	393	392	391	390
389	388	387	386	385	384	383	382	381	380
379	378	377	376	375	374	373	372	371	370
369	368	367	366	365	364	363	362	361	360
359	358	357	356	355	354	353	352	351	350

Page 25
1. 10, 40, 51, 31, 55
2. 14, 20, 23, 13, 10
3. 6, 16, 50, 23, 44
4. 10, 44, 64, 22, 50
5. 22, 40, 83, 32, 55

Page 26
1. 3, 51, 13, 40, 22
2. 1, 10, 52, 51, 16
3. 12, 20, 2, 5, 31
4. 40, 1, 15, 72, 45
5. 30, 11, 63, 21, 8

Page 27
1. 64, 15, 84, 5, 42
2. 0, 53, 10, 54, 22
3. 13, 13, 51, 31, 21
4. 21, 70, 10, 57, 11
5. 23, 34, 33, 71, 21

Page 28

449	448	447	446	445	444	443	442	441	440
439	438	437	436	435	434	433	432	431	430
429	428	427	426	425	424	423	422	421	420
419	418	417	416	415	414	413	412	411	410
409	408	407	406	405	404	403	402	401	400

Page 29

499	498	497	496	495	494	493	492	491	490
489	488	487	486	485	484	483	482	481	480
479	478	477	476	475	474	473	472	471	470
469	468	467	466	465	464	463	462	461	460
459	458	457	456	455	454	453	452	451	450

Page 30
1. 741, 153, 507, 584, 624
2. 375, 130, 238, 710, 50
3. 114, 521, 321, 114, 550
4. 450, 212, 521, 242, 630
5. 430, 412, 121, 200, 112

Page 31
1. 121, 343, 111, 301, 747
2. 136, 111, 532, 206, 253
3. 53, 122, 141, 124, 51
4. 164, 221, 316, 246, 179

Page 32
1. 452−241=211
2. 567−325=242
3. 286−160=126
4. 724−510=214

Page 33

549	548	547	546	545	544	543	542	541	540
539	538	537	536	535	534	533	532	531	530
529	528	527	526	525	524	523	522	521	520
519	518	517	516	515	514		512	511	510
509	508	507	506	505		503	502	501	500

Page 34

599	598	597	596		594	593	592	591	590
589	588	587		585	584	583	582	581	580
579	578	577		575	574	573	572	571	570
569	568		566	565	564	563	562	561	560
559	558		556	555	554	553	552	551	550

Page 35

	648	647	646	645	644	643	642	641	640
9	638	637	636	635	634	633	632	631	630
629	628	627	626	625	624	623	622	621	620
619	618	617	616	615	614	613	612	611	610
609	608	607	606	605	604	603	602	601	600

Page 36

699	698	697	696	695	694	693	692	691	690
689	688	687	686	685	684	683	682	681	680
679	678	677	676	675	674	673	672	671	670
669	668	667	666	665	664	663	662	661	660
659	658	657	656	655	654	653	652	651	650

Page 37

1. $\frac{1}{4}$ 2. $\frac{2}{4}$ 3. $\frac{3}{8}$ 4. $\frac{1}{3}$

Page 38

1. $\frac{3}{4}$ 2. $\frac{1}{2}$ 3. $\frac{7}{8}$

4. $\frac{1}{3}$ 5. $\frac{1}{5}$ 6. $\frac{4}{10}$

Page 39

1. 19, 19, 17, 29, 57
2. 59, 46, 38, 12, 17
3. 29, 9, 8, 19, 15
4. 28, 17, 37, 39, 18
5. 48, 7, 38, 49, 57

Page 40

1. 68, 45, 29, 17, 14
2. 48, 5, 14, 11, 14
3. 26, 39, 46, 64, 62
4. 37, 7, 49, 9, 14
5. 9, 19, 59, 66, 32

Page 41

1. 28, 37, 59, 58, 13
2. 18, 12, 36, 35, 42
3. 29, 19, 46, 53, 18
4. 15, 38, 57, 18, 68
5. 8, 17, 5, 19, 23

Page 42

1. 16, 13, 26, 16, 21
2. 12, 11, 14, 45, 33
3. 8, 3, 50, 39, 3
4. 18, 8, 10, 28, 69
5. 16, 10, 18, 59, 36

Page 43

1. 20, 19, 7, 12, 33
2. 68, 40, 28, 18, 47
3. 9, 23, 23, 29, 10
4. 18, 42, 17, 14, 6
5. 40, 40, 66, 31, 5

Page 44

1. ⑫ ⑫ 4, 3, ⑫ 11
2. 38, 12, ⑰ ⑰ 58, ⑰
3. ㉖ ㉖ 18, 1, ㉖ ㉖
4. 25, 21, ㉚ 2, ㉚ ㉚

Answer Pages

Page 45
1. 42
− 14
28

2. 67
−41
26

3. 52
− 14
38

4. 21
− 18
3

Page 46
1. 84
− 68
16

2. 97
− 48
49

3. 78
− 29
49

4. 86
− 19
67

Page 47
1. 35, (13), 32, 17, (13), 4
2. (42), 48, 40, 20, 14, (42)
3. (3)(3)(3)(3)(3), 9
4. 76, (25), (25), 35, (25), (25)

Page 48
1. 489, 149, 290, 199, 297
2. 187, 842, 175, 182, 519
3. 394, 308, 398, 209, 575
4. 278, 802, 625, 491, 408
5. 107, 109, 232, 833, 159

Page 49
1. 469, 84, 516, 396, 149
2. 688, 738, 305, 148, 478
3. 106, 146, 167, 113, 186
4. 168, 90, 382, 31, 71
5. 77, 245, 767, 103, 347

Page 50
1. 139, 277, 110, 193, 599
2. 11, 80, 286, 312, 99
3. 105, 49, 588, 403, 201
4. 100, 255, 155, 2, 198
5. 234, 83, 200, 13, 494

Page 51
600, 400, 500, 600, 300, 800
He gave away 1,900 pencils.

Page 52
$5 − 3 = 2$
$12 − 4 = 8$
$10 − 8 = 2$
Answers will vary.

Page 53
10, 10, 9, 13
1. a
2. c
3. b, c, d
4. d
5. c
6. d

Page 54
1. 2, 2

2. 4, 4

3. 4, 4

Page 55
Elephant a has 0 peanuts.
Elephant b has 3 peanuts.
(square around elephant a)

Page 56–57
Answers will vary.

Page 58
1. 5   2   3
    4   2   2
    1   0   1

2. 13   4   9
    3   2   1
   10   2   8

3. 45 38   7
    4   3   1
   41 35   6

4. 97 77 20
   15   6   9
   82 71 11

Answer Pages

Page 59
70, 60, 50
60 – 10, 50 – 10
60, 50, 40
Rule: subtract 10

73, 64, 55
64 – 9, 55 – 9
64, 55, 46
Rule: subtract 9

76, 68, 60
18 – 8, 60 – 8
68, 60, 52
Rule: subtract 8

Page 60
9, 40, 43, 48, 34, 22, 42
21, 30, 46, 26, 1, 51, 44
20, 50, 40, 32, 72, 31, 41
9, 42, 33, 35, 30, 22, 42
23, 22, 10, 24, 20, 49, 44
71, 60, 36, 25, 27, 21, 31

Page 61
22, 4
Rule: subtract 18

20
Rule: subtract 25

29, 12
Rule: subtract 17

15, 6
Rule: subtract 9

10
Rule: subtract 19

Page 62
Answers will vary.

Page 63
50 – 30 = 20; 90 – 10 = 80; 70 – 40 = 30
➜ swamp

Page 64
1. 200, 100, 0
Rule: Decrease the number in the 100s
place by 1.

2. 20, 10, 0
Rule: Decrease the number in the 10s
place by 1.

3. 12, 11, 10
Rule: Decrease the number in the 1s
place by 1.

4. 28, 26, 24
Rule: Decrease the number in the 1s
place by 2.

5. 200, 0
Rule: Decrease the number in the 100s
place by 2.

6. 201, 101, 1
Rule: Decrease the number in the 100s
place by 1.

7. 80, 75, 70
Rule: Decrease the number in the 1s
place by 5.

Page 65
1. 14<19   16<17   12>8   17<18
2. 10>9   11>6   0<1   15>7
Marbles: White — because there are
more white marbles in the bag.

Page 66
The picture is a tepee!

Page 67
Lori had the most left over. Her two
goldfish cost $2.00 together. ($5–$2=$3)

Answer Pages

Page 68
1. 8:15, or 15 minutes after 8 o'clock
2. 1:40, or 40 minutes after 1 o'clock
3. 11:20, or 20 minutes after 11 o'clock
4. 1:15, or 15 minutes after 11 o'clock

Page 69
The answer is 15.

Page 70
Across:
1. three   **2.** school   **3.** subtraction
4. equation   **5.** nine   **6.** solve
Down:
1. two   **2.** eleven   **3.** clock
4. number   **5.** sixteen   **6.** hands

Page 71

Page 72
1. 42   **2.** ⑤   **3.** 22   **4.** ⑨
5. 60   **6.** 46   **7.** 0   **8.** 80
9. 34   **10.** 14

Notes

5 Five things I'm
thankful for:

1. _____
2. _____
3. _____
4. _____
5. _____